To four Be Loved women:
My mother, Jeanne, who fought for my dreams,
My wife, Jill, who chose me from all the men in the world,
Jill's mom, Nancy, who modeled for me the way of love,
My fan, Jeanne, who gave herself everyday to love.

Contents

Acknowledgements

I am so grateful to my wife Jill, whose loving touch and consistent support has made the writing of this book possible. She is my friend, wife, counselor, and lover these past 27 years.

My five incredible children have blessed me tremendously! Edward—who lives with courage and excellence; Jessica—who lives everyday for God with boldness and faith; Mary Lee—who makes life beautiful and full of adventure; Lukas—whose tender heart moves me to be more compassionate; and Joshua—who swings for the fence every time and believes that nothing is impossible. Having their hearts and being a part of their story is a treasure to me.

I want to thank my TEAM at the Power of the Blessing Ministries, Jimmy and Pattie, Dac and Donna, Dale and Marianne, Wayne and Kate, Jim West and Barnabas group. You have made such a difference in my life.

I want to thank Dr. Rob Johnson for the difference his friendship has made on my life, and my friends and counselors—Ron, Eleanor, and Michael.

I also want to thank Brian Holloway, whose friendship and inspiration for the last 30 years has given me the courage to go for it and make a difference.

I can't forget my California family, who has always been there—the Andersen's, the Nelsons, the Andrews, and Nanny and Ole.

I also want to thank my two sisters, Cindy and Chan, and my brother, Dan, who I wish didn't live across the country.

My Aunt Barbara and David, and cousins, Maurice, Nina, Nanette, Walter, and Chris—you are in my heart.

I want to thank Jason Chatraw, who believed in me and pursued me to broadcast this message, and my church, the Stadium Vineyard—there is not enough room to write all of the names of those who have loved me into the pastor I am becoming.

I also want to thank my associate pastor Glenn Rees, who has loved me and supported me for so many years. It has been an honor to serve next to him.

Finally, I want to thank the 200,000-plus people who read my first book and have given themselves to blessing their kids and making a difference in the next generation.

Ed Tandy McGlasson

EXPERIENCING THE POWER
OF GOD'S BLESSING
IN YOUR LIFE

ampelōn
PUBLISHING

ISBN: 978-0-9798104-0-4

Printed in the United States of America

Requests for information should be addressed to:
Ampelon Publishing
PO Box 140675
Boise, ID 83714

Visit us on the web at: www.ampelonpublishing.com
Connect with Ed's ministry at: www.PowerOfTheBlessing.com

To Be Loved

After a long day of work, I walked into our home to the sound of a loud commotion and the smell of an unidentified burning object. Before I took two steps inside the door, my wife ran to meet me.

"Come see what *your* son Luke has done!" she said, obviously so distressed over his actions that she momentarily disowned him.

I walked into our carpeted garage and immediately realized what both the commotion and the awful smell were all about. At age nine, Luke had discovered a new talent with my heat gun. Through experimentation, he learned that if you held the heat gun about an inch above the carpet, it would melt the carpet fibers together. Just to make sure that we all remembered his eureka moment, he used his new artistic tool to spell out "Lucas" on the carpet. Oblivious to the frantic screams of his mother, he was still finishing up his masterpiece when I arrived.

When he saw me walk in the room, he looked up at me as a huge grin spread across his face. "What do you think, dad?" he asked, anxiously anticipating my response.

My initial thought was to rip his head off. How could he do such a thing?! But I waited a moment before saying anything—and while doing so I looked down and realized just how proud Luke was of his artistic talent. Finally, much to my wife's dismay, I replied, "You didn't finish the 's'."

Haven't we all been there before, desperate to get our father's attention? What's in us that compels us to sometimes go to the extreme to get our dad to notice us whenever we feel hidden or disconnected? I believe God made us that way. He made us with a longing to be adored. He gave us a yearning to be loved. He made us want to be seen and appreciated. And He made us for His smile.

Once we catch God's smile over our lives and understand that He is a God who sings and celebrates our lives, life changes for us. Living under His smile, we move from grasping for every possible moment of affirmation to understanding that we have already arrived.

Regardless of the depths you have sunken to or the

heights you have ascended, my heart's desire is for you to see God smiling over your life. I want you to understand the power of God's blessing—how God's smile is fixed over your life and that you no longer have to work to get His approval or attention. I want you to capture what it means to be loved by God and how you can embrace His unconditional love and acceptance. And I want you to understand how to help others experience this for themselves.

Let's unravel this truth together.

CHAPTER ONE

Daddy, Do You See Me?

In my first book *The Difference a Father Makes*, I shared how my daughters used to hold fashion shows in front of my office to get my attention, hungry for me to tell them how beautiful they were. As a father, I absolutely delighted in those opportunities to reinforce my love and passion for my girls, but I have encountered many women who never received the validation they craved from their fathers.

After reading my book, one woman wrote me to share the pain in her experience growing up. Though her father was physically present, he was emotionally distant. After he came home from work each day and plopped down in front of the television, she would put on different outfits and stand in front of him to get his attention. Instead of taking a moment to notice her or compliment her, he was gruff. "Daddy, do you see me?" she would ask, to which her father replied, "Get out of my way! You're blocking my view!"

She wrote: "I remember as a young girl just wanting one look from my dad, just to have a moment like you had with your daughter when you looked into her eyes and told her how beautiful she was. I was so grateful to read your story and now I know I have a Father in heaven who sees me, adores me, who calls me beautiful. It was like the wound that I was carrying all these years started to be healed when I knew that Jesus came to bring me a new Father."

This question—"Do you see me?"—is one each of us has asked our parents as well as significant others in our lives. In sharing my story and this message over the years, I have realized that God created something in us as children that yearns for approval and acceptance. When that approval is missing in our lives, it becomes easy for us to attempt to fill that need by performing for others we seek to impress.

The reality for so many people I meet is that they have lived under this big question mark in their lives because most of their fathers didn't know what to do—because they, too, lived under the same question mark. A big question mark that can be summed up by a series of questions:

* Who am I?
* Am I someone to be loved, appreciated and respected?

* Am I somebody you want?

There aren't many things harder in life than giving all of yourself to gain the approval of someone who doesn't even realize that you want it.

Always Performing

After suffering a terrible knee injury in practice one day while playing college football—and then experiencing a miraculous healing from God the next, I came back to my dorm room overwhelmed at the mercy of God in my life while at the same time thinking about my future in football. When science and the miraculous meet, our world-view shifts. Whether slightly or drastically, it shifts and we all know it. The God who I used to think was merely a religious symbol was actually real, living, and He wanted a relationship with me. His unconditional love started challenging everything I had done in my life up to that point. When Jesus said, "I am the way, the truth and the life," He didn't add that His unconditional mercy was going to turn my world upside down and heal me from the inside out. Salvation had saved my life, but my heart was torn because up to that point being a professional football player was the only way I was able to measure my life.

I started thinking about all the work, the time, the sacrifice, the injuries, and the priority of football above all else. Suddenly, I was facing the possibility that my dream had hit a wall that I wouldn't be able to power through. What would I do then? Where would I go? Who would I be? My whole identity, my whole sense of self was wrapped up in being a gridiron hero.

When I opened the door to my room, much to my surprise, I found a rehabilitation machine sitting like a metal island in the middle of my room. Upon hearing the news of my injury, my mother rushed to Youngstown, Ohio, from our home in Maryland, bought an exercise machine to help with my rehab and put it in my room with a note on it: "Son, I believe in you. Your dreams are still going to come true. Use this. Love, Mom."

Her words brought tears to my eyes. They still do today. My mom really believed in me! My mom had a powerful ability to speak life and encouragement into my world. She was my greatest fan. But underneath, this underscored a troubling dilemma brewing deep beneath the surface in my heart: I felt the need to constantly push myself to perform for the approval and validation of others.

Being the son of a military hero who died while serving his country contributed to my self-induced pressure to achieve, to become someone. I still remember the words of my mom as she desperately tried to give hope and meaning to such a tragic event in our lives. She would say, "Ed, God wouldn't have let your father die unless He had something great for you to do." Those words drove me to live a life worthy of my father's sacrifice. I couldn't fail his legacy. Out of her desire to love and support me in the context of such a monumental loss, my mom inadvertently fueled the flame of drivenness to "win" at everything I attempted.

By only talking about my dad's strengths, my mom framed him in my young mind as a superhero. And a super-hero is a mighty tough act to follow. I can tell you because I've tried my best! And it's exhausting. It also left precious little room for me to be myself, to accept that I was put together with a particular blend of talents, passions, abilities, foibles, imperfections and limitations.

My mom's attempt to frame God's purposes for my life, indeed to place an umbrella of blessing over my life, inadvertently became one of myriad examples of how I became a prisoner to perfect performance, a standard that I will never be able to meet in this lifetime.

At multiple times and places in my life, unable to achieve that ideal, I found myself on my knees, weeping out of a deep sense of shame, embarrassment and inadequacy. I just couldn't measure up to the bar that had been set for me—even though it was a bar in many ways that I had set for myself. Not only was I struggling with self-hatred around my inability to create the heroic life and identity for which I strove, but I was also even more ashamed of having let down my father's legacy. Even as I write this, I shake my head at the level of sorrow I would feel at those times, unable to replicate a persona that I now know never even existed.

No Fear

Since evidently one over-idealized role model wasn't enough, my mom remarried another Naval academy graduate, Dan McGlasson. One story my step-dad told often captured his motivational style: After discovering his son's fear of swimming, his father took him to a bridge that crossed a small local river and threw him over the railing, shouting, "Sink or swim! Live or die trying, son! It is up to you!" My step-dad would then tell me, "Well, son, I made it! My father wouldn't accept my being afraid of anything, so that goes for you, too!" Another stitch had been added to my superman costume.

I found myself reacting to that by never letting anyone see that I hurt or was afraid. I thought if I always appeared to have it together then I would be accepted. For years I played along with the bravado that men do by bragging about my father's toughness.

As well as being a great motivator, my stepfather was my first football coach. One of the things I admire about him was that he hardly ever missed my football games. He would drive for hours to see my games and then drive home to be back at work by Monday morning.

I remember my first practice on his youth football team. Nobody wanted to play center and my step-dad looked at me and said, "You get the job." *How about a vote?* I thought. Not on his team. Later that day he became so frustrated with my fear of being hit by the other guys on the team that he stopped practice and said, "Son, I want you to run at me and hit me as hard as you can." I didn't want to. I was afraid I'd get hurt. His voice grew and the next thing I knew I was running at him. Then came a blow from his right forearm and the lights went out. The next thing I remember was hearing him say, "Are you all right, son? How many fingers do you see? Listen to me, son! There is no reason to be afraid. No one out here is as big and strong as me, and if you can take my hit, you can take anyone's." I thought, *What the heck are you talking about? You just knocked me out!* You could hear the other players running for cover, afraid he was going to holler at them next. He was trying to love me the way his father loved him—I am just grateful that there were no bridges nearby.

The loss of my father, the words of my mom, and the

drive of my stepfather taught me to walk with a John Wayne swagger and perform for every crowd I could find. The only smile I knew came when the score was in my favor at the end of the game.

When I eventually made it to the NFL, football's biggest stage, I continued to feed that need—or so I thought! Everything was fine until Joe Klecko, the New York Jets All-Pro defensive tackle, ran over me in practice day in and day out. He took great pleasure in pounding this rookie into the turf. My claim to fame my rookie year was an article in *The New York Times* titled, "Portrait of a Rookie," which featured a picture of me lying on my back after being run over by Joe.

The Call

I was in training camp with the Philadelphia Eagles in 1983 when the call of God came to me. I had one of those sleepless nights, an easy task during camp where you wake up each morning wondering if you are going to make it through another day without being cut. The team began with 125 players at training camp before being trimmed to a 45-man final roster. It makes you neurotic to say the least. One of those sleepless nights in particular led me to the field to spend some time with God. He interrupted my walk with a statement: "Ed, I want you to leave football and preach the Gospel." I thought, *No, not now!* I said, "Lord, don't you know how much money I gave the church last year?" He was not impressed. I have since learned that when God calls us, He is not asking for permission—He is letting us know where we are headed. All I can say is sheer terror filled my heart. "But I am a football player, Lord!" I pleaded. "Who is going to listen to a football player?"

Much like today, pro athletes were sought after to speak at churches—and there were not many of us. Once while sitting next to a pastor on the platform, I turned to him and said, "I think I have a word from God to share from Scripture." The pastor sternly looked at me and said, "That is my job. Besides you are only a football player. You have three minutes to share your testimony. Right?" I thought, *Lord, you want me to go to this group? No way!*

Life as a pastor was worlds apart from life as a football hero. As a pastor, one moment you feel like a hero; the next moment, you're judged and vilified. If your identity and sense of well being is dependent on the assessment of others, it can be terribly stifling to your self-worth.

My early years of ministry were marked by this internal struggle. Though I was in ministry for the glory of God and serving Him, I found the transition difficult from being a celebrity and hearing people beg for my autograph to hearing people say, "Excuse me, pastor, but you're just a human being. I don't need your help." The hardest days came when I learned that someone decided to leave the church. It devastated me. Sometimes it was the Lord sending them on, but many times it came as a result of relationship issues and my own inability to be a good leader. As I reflect on my early days of ministry, I realize it was difficult for people to relate to a pastor who always appeared to have it together and never showed his pain and failure.

Running people over in the NFL didn't give me much training for my new job of pastoring. The more I tried to become a servant the more I became depressed. On the football field you can always tell whether you are winning by looking at the scoreboard; there wasn't such a clear win-loss record in the ministry. Most of the feedback I received was ambivalent at best and after finding myself more and more depressed, a friend of mine suggested I see a psychiatrist.

I remember bristling at the notion I needed help. *There isn't anything wrong with me,* I thought, which is almost always the first sign that something most certainly is wrong. Finally, I decided to call him and asked him to play a round of golf with me. To which he intuitively replied, "So, you're afraid of seeing a shrink?" We both laughed and headed off to a golf course in southern California. Once we arrived at the driving range, I began describing some of my feelings—

discouragement, being stuck in my job, angry, wondering how I could be loved one moment and hated the next.

As we started the back nine, he asked me the question that helped frame my journey: "Have you always been performing in front of a crowd?" His question resonated so deeply with me that my hand started shaking. I could hardly put the ball on the tee and hooked my next shot into a lake. I then asked him, "Is this how you beat everybody in golf, by asking penetrating questions that shake them to the core?" Rattled by his question, I played the worst nine holes of golf I had played in a long time.

When we came to the final hole, he looked at me and said, "You know what the secret is?"

I said, "No, what's that?"

"You have to change your focus to an audience of One," he said. "You have to quit seeking approval from audiences who are not even watching. If you were to receive an award from the president and you could ask any five people, living or dead, to your table to watch you get that award, who would you place at that table?"

The names came to mind immediately. He then responded, "That's the audience you've been trying to impress. I've learned that no matter how hard you try, you can never please all the people around that table at the same time. The solution is to stop trying."

Emptying Your Table

So, who's sitting at your table? Whose approval are you striving to earn in the way you live your life? The trick is to unseat those people at the table and put God there alone. When I began to make that transition from performing for the people seated at my table to serving God, it started a journey that connected me with a deep, intimate, daily walk with the only One who can fulfill the desires of my heart. Not only that, I got His Father, too.

Whether the audience is your boss, your family or your friends, you've been waiting for someone to let you know that you've arrived. Without experiencing that deep validation in your heart, you live a life of endless pursuit toward a goal line that never arrives. Even when you get the applause of those around you, your happiness and validation are only present when you are winning. What happens the rest of the time?

A friend of mine coached a Little League team that had a kid on the roster one year who simply did not care one iota about baseball. For his disinterest in sports in general, and particularly baseball, he earned the nickname "Dan, the Daisy Picker." It was quite literal, too, as Dan once was picking flowers on the field in the middle of a soccer game as a herd of players thundered past him.

Little League rules require that each child play at least one inning in the field and get at least one at bat. Realizing that Dan didn't want to be on the field and other players there were begging for playing time, the coach played him the minimum amount. This infuriated Dan's dad, who was a prominent member of the community. He sternly told the coach he needed to play Dan and that his son should actually be starting.

The next week against one of the weaker teams in the league, my friend, in an effort to assuage Dan's father, decided to let Dan start and get his playing time over with up front. But the decision turned out to be disastrous—or fortuitous if you're looking at it from Dan's perspective.

Playing in the less-than-glorious position of left field, Dan was hardly ready when the second batter of the game hit a fly ball in his direction. Dan had his legs crossed and was humming as he looked at the ground when the ball began traveling in his direction. Noticing Dan's lack of attention, the crowd began screaming and pleading with Dan to look up and catch the ball. Positioned perfectly, Dan didn't have to move. The ball was coming down … right … on … top … of … him. All he had to do was stick his glove out. He didn't.

Disoriented, Dan stood in awe of the ball coming in his direction until it crashed from the sky on top of his foot, sending him clutching his cleat and writhing in pain. A doctor in the stands rushed onto the field and delivered the bad news. Dan had a broken foot and would be out for at least six weeks.

Other than a broken foot, this scene is played out over and over on sports fields across the country each week. Instead of blessing their sons and daughters for who God has made them to be, parents drive their kids to become the somebody they always strove to become, despite their lack of success. Not feeling that they have arrived themselves, fathers, believing that performance determines identity, drive their kids toward athletic attainment.

Maybe you are Dan, the Daisy Picker. Maybe your parents forced their dreams for your life on you, dreams that were never yours and still aren't. Maybe you have spent your entire life trying to earn the approval of someone who will never give it to you because you're not shaped to be a baseball player or a concert violinist or a Pulitzer Prize winning scientist. Maybe God designed you to be a teacher or a coach or an artist.

You could be in the wrong position in life because you allowed someone other than God to name you. I used to see that in the NFL all the time. There were players who spent their entire collegiate careers trying to become something they thought they were supposed to become, only to achieve it and discover that it's not what they wanted. Does that ring true for you? No matter how much money you earn or how many accolades you receive, you never feel like you arrive. You're constantly pushing, manipulating, pressing—so you can come out a winner.

For the rest of this book, we'll be going on a journey from performance to approval, from pushing a rock uphill to receiving the blessing and freedom that God has for everyone of us to live in. We're going to empty your table of all those people whose approval you're trying to earn. You're going to get to that place where you can live from approval and not for it, where you can live from a deep sense of acceptance rather than trying to prove yourself with the mantra, "If I just do that harder and better, I'll arrive!"

While flying home from a recent trip, a fellow seat-mate gave me the greatest definition of retirement. He said, "Retirement is doing something that you love and were made for." Given that definition, are you ready to retire right now? Here is the truth: God shaped you to live with stimulating roles that fire your energy, curiosity, and passion, and which fill you with gratitude for the opportunity. He designed you to live out of His smile and approval, and He has embedded gifts and talents in you that define what He made you for.

So, whether you're "Dan, the Daisy Picker" or the next Michael Jordan, or you're learning to swim from bridges or the little girl standing in front of your dad saying, "Daddy, do you see me?", there is a better way. There is healing from the wounds with which we live everyday. It's the way of the smile of the Father and learning how to embrace His unconditional love and acceptance.

CHAPTER TWO

The Frown:
Understanding Our Wounds

In order to truly understand how to live with God's smile over our lives and experience the power of His blessing over our lives, we must understand the place from which we came—a place littered with broken promises and dreams. All of us are desperate to understand how to live in a place of complete freedom and be who God has created us to be, but getting there seems like a country in a foreign land a thousand miles away. This is not a journey that is completed overnight. It takes patience and commitment, but it begins with an understanding of where we are now and how our past has influenced our present. It took time to unseat the audience at my table, too.

Both my stepfather and mother had a lasting impact on my life, helping me build a ladder to my dreams. However, as I worked hard to pursue my ultimate goal of starting in the NFL, it was as if the purpose of my life, for both me and my parents, morphed into "all or nothing"— either the dream or bust. Although we shared this dream to play in the NFL, I began to feel captive to the dream.

The Call ... Continued

There is more to my story from Eagles training camp. The next day while performing a routine pass blocking drill, I planted on my right leg and it buckled under me. Team trainers rushed me to the doctor, who quickly left the room to have a meeting with team personnel. The doctor came back and told me that though I had injured my knee it wasn't bad enough to necessitate surgery. They entered me in a six-hour-a-day rehabilitation program—and curiously, I could sense an attitude shift with the coaches. Ten days later the doctor came back and tested my knee, pronouncing I was ready for practice. I thought that was strange since I had only been walking in the pool and had not even run a step.

Though my knee was still swollen, the trainer taped it up and off to the field I went for practice. During warm ups I could barely run. I told the coach, and he said, "Don't worry about it. The doctor passed you and I need you to play center." I broke from the huddle and lined up against Charley Johnson, the same player I was blocking when my knee collapsed two weeks earlier. I snapped the ball to the quarterback and tried to push off my knee and fell to the ground. I ran another play and my knee collapsed again.

The doctor came out and took me away to the training room and gave me three ice bags and told me to report to the training room in the morning. What happened the next day was one of the biggest shocks of my life.

Upon reporting to the trainer, he told me to go see team management. I walked into the general manager's office and he delivered the devastating news. "Ed," he said, "we have decided to release you from the team." I couldn't believe my ears. The NFL, the organization I had sold out for, was going to sell me out. Being completely exasperated, I said, "You can't do that. I am still hurt and it is against my contract for you to cut me."

He then said, "Listen, Ed, we know that you are a good Christian, and you won't sue us. And if you should try that, I will make sure that you never play football in the NFL again." My heart was completely broken. The very dream to which I had given myself had been stolen away from me by a dishonest man. (It later came out that the owner had a gambling problem and was cutting every possible expense. I happened to be one of those cutbacks.)

A good Christian? I thought. After thinking about what he said, I went home and started to rehabilitate my knee. To make matters worse, my wife and I had just had our first son, Edward, and we had little money in the bank.

Three months later, the Super Bowl bound Los Angeles Rams called me and asked if I would be interested in playing in the playoffs with the team. When I went in for the physical, I couldn't run well. The team doctor looked at my knee and said, "Ed, you have torn your cartilage and need surgery. The Eagles did you wrong." I ended up paying for my own surgery, pushing me further into depression.

To God, the timing was perfect. I thought, *Did this happen because I hesitated with God the night before when He called me. Is He punishing me?* I had a lot to learn about who the Father really is (and still do). He is not petty; He doesn't punish us to prove a point. My own projection of God being angry with me and His blowing out my knee came from my performance mentality. I also thought He was disappointed with me because my first reaction was fear. I was waiting for the bridge He was getting ready to toss me from.

As I entered the ministry, I held this same mindset toward success. I thought if the church wasn't growing exponentially, I was a loser. Almost immediately, I found myself entombed in a performance-driven lifestyle, an endless place of never feeling like I had arrived, and like my efforts were never good enough. Instead of taking the time to actually build my ministry with patience and love, I found myself diverting my attention to activities where I could score quick "wins," even though it sometimes meant ignoring the more authentic needs of my congregation. It's always easier to get a quick pat on the back than guiding projects—or people—through their inevitable developmental ups and downs. In the end, I realized I was performing to obtain love rather than as a result of feeling loved.

Stirring up the Wound

Once while I was traveling to Germany to speak at a conference, I met a pastor who stood up and spoke passionately about the power of God. He shared how God wanted to give people gifts and empower them to do His work. However, I felt as if he was trying to convince himself of this truth rather than speak from his own hard-earned experience. Something was wrong.

While having lunch with this pastor the following day, I had an image of him as a boy waiting at a party for someone to arrive. When I asked him about it, he began crying. He then shared from his pain that the image was from one of his birthday parties—and he was waiting for his dad. "My dad never came to my birthday," he told me. "He was a German soldier and a very hard man. He never came to one of my parties or gave me a gift." We both realized how this pastor's relationship with his father had impacted him on so many levels, including his view of God. While he believed intellectually that God gave people gifts, he struggled to experience it for himself because he had never been given any gifts by his own father.

Most people can grasp the concept of Jesus and see Him as a patient and loving man. But when the word "father" comes up, it stirs up wounds inside many people. So many of us have come from homes where our dads didn't know how to lovingly affirm and speak blessing into our lives because they were held captive by those same question marks in their own lives: Who am I? And what am I on earth for? Where is the goal line?

The Day the Smile Was Lost

The German pastor's experience or your own story is not a novel one; this has been going on in slightly different guises for ages. Thousands upon thousands of fathers live with doubts, self-critical thoughts, and nagging questions hanging over their heads, leaving them unable to establish healthy and effective relationships with their children. When and where did this all go wrong?

Contrary to what you might think, this is not all about your dad. There's another "father" who has spent all of his resources trying to keep us from experiencing the blessing of God. The Bible calls him the "father of lies" or Satan. The day he successfully coerced humanity into making sinful choices was the day the smile of the Father was lost over creation—although thankfully not lost forever.

In the early days of the Garden of Eden, the Bible tells us that God was present and walked with Adam and Eve in the "cool of the evening." (Genesis 3:8) They had a relationship that was loving and real. This was a dad enjoying his children. No agendas, no expectations—just a parent and child enjoying each other's company in shared respect and honor.

There wasn't a laundry list of rules for the Garden—just one: Do not eat off the tree of knowledge of good and evil. Simple enough, right?

But in the midst of exploring the beauty and fruitfulness of the Garden, Eve stumbled across that one particular tree and Satan was conveniently right there to greet her. He invited her to partake of the fruit, promising that her eyes would be opened to her own power. In other words, "Eve, eat this fruit and you won't need anyone to tell you how to live your life—you can make your own choices; you can be self-sufficient."

This offer was irresistible, and each of us probably would have done the same thing in Eve's position. Instead of simply tempting her to break a rule, the "father of lies" was tempting her with the offer of independence from God. She could make her own rules if she ate the fruit. God, the Father, who so freely gave blessing and life, lost his children to the "father of lies" in a moment as both Adam and Eve caved into that now universal temptation. The curse that subsequently befell humanity was that instead of having the opportunity to reap boundless fruit and enjoy an unhindered and direct relationship with the heart of God, life got tough. Humanity would have to work the land to gather a harvest.

However, the curse was far more sinister than that. Because of Adam and Eve's choice to try and become like a god, they also triggered a standard for measuring winners and losers. No longer was man to be accepted solely based on God's inherent love for him; he now had to earn it based on unerring compliance with God's rules—a virtually impossible standard for human beings, an unattainable metric for winning and losing.

The curse set in motion that day said this: "Your performance names you." No longer could people just enjoy God's creation and experience a freedom in relationship with Him. Our success would depend on how hard we worked and be based on our achievements.

How many people do you meet who define themselves by what they do for a living? They find their identity in how well they perform. Maybe that describes you as well. Maybe you feel like there is no smile over your life from anyone, just endless days of pushing your rock up a hill that has no reachable summit. That life is punishing. And exhausting. And it is death to dreams and passion.

Will Someone Love Me for Who I am?

While speaking in Denver I met an 83-year-old Jewish man who walked forward at one of my conferences and said with tears brimming in his eyes, "Ed, I have made every dollar a man could make. I bought every car I ever wanted and have owned many homes. But the only thing I ever wanted was my dad to tell me one time that he loved me and was proud of me!" When this man's time for Bar mitzvah came, his dad was a no-show. Instead his father was at work, his eyes on a distant goal line that had nothing to do with his own authentic needs or desires, much less those of his adolescent son. I wept with that grown son as I watched the love of the Heavenly Father descend on his broken heart and give him the blessing for which he had longed.

For many people, the gaping wound left by Adam and Eve remains today. This is the wound: We don't feel recognized, approved or honored for who we are. Instead we feel ignored, anxious, and insecure, striving to get someone to notice us. We are looking for someone who can make us feel understood, valued and sufficient, someone whose loving acceptance can unlock us from our treadmill of effort. We silently scream, "Will someone ever love me for who I am?"

Remember, I said that the smile over creation was lost, but not forever. God, the Father, is not like our flawed earthly fathers. He really is good and just—and He devoted the most precious thing He had—His son, Jesus—to help regain that smile over creation. Jesus came into the world to reverse the curse, to bring back the blessing we forfeited. He came to restore the smile over all of humanity—the same smile under which Jesus actively lived His life. Jesus came to restore the smile of the Father.

The Message paraphrases King David like this: "You pile blessings on him; you make him glad when You smile" (Psalm 21:6). That is the life that Jesus woke up to every morning, the life of a person who knew that He was His Father's beloved, a person who possessed a quiet assurance that He was intimately known, loved and valued. I think we all wish we awoke to that message imprinted on our hearts.

That is the same life God wants to give us. I love how *The Message* paraphrases Ephesians 1:6: "He wanted us to enter into the celebration of his lavish gift-giving by the hand of his beloved Son."

Understanding the Heart of the Father

What does God really think about you? Consider this verse in the Old Testament:

The Lord your God is with you, he is mighty to save. He will take great delight in you, he will quiet you with his love, he will rejoice over you with singing. (Zephaniah 3:17, NIV)

This verse brings a smile to my face every time I think about it. God actually rejoices over me! He loves me that much. The father of lies has tricked us into believing that God is angry with us, that he wants to punish us and that we can never be good enough to be loved by Him. But the truth is that when God thinks about us, His love is so intense that it causes Him to burst into song!

Even as I am writing this book, my computer Internet browser is linked to a website that gives updates of the professional golf tournament my oldest son is playing in. I can honestly say that my heart has been captured for my kids and that in itself is a miracle. It is hard for me to do anything when my kids are competing in sports, leading worship, living out their dreams and I am not able to be with them. I have had times when my heart burst into song over their lives.

In one of those song moments, I was so captured in praying for Edward that I started dancing and singing in my office. Hearing the bellowing in my office, my staff walked in and saw me performing my lovesick musical. When they caught me, I started laughing at myself. After they left, the voice of the Lord interrupted my song and said, "Ed, as much as you love your kids, it doesn't compare to the love I have for you. I can't wait for you to hear the song I am singing over you."

From Wounds to Trust

As we begin to unravel the truth about how God feels about us, there is a common place from which we must begin, a place that many of us are tentative to tread near. That place? It's a place of trust. As Brennan Manning puts it, "Trust is our gift back to God, and he finds it so enchanting that Jesus died for the love of it."

Try to put away all the distrust that you have about your earthly father. You might even have to put away distrust that you have for God. On some level , we've all been disappointed by something on this earth and have taken our questions up with God. In fact, this is healthy to do. But our questions—answered or not—are not an excuse to cast a leery eye on anything we associate with God, the Father.

In my journey with God, I've learned that He gives me every single thing I need to be who He has called me to be and to do everything He has called me to do. It's as if He has said, "Ed, here are two choices. You can live out of My grace and power, or you can spend your life trying to recreate My grace and power. Which one will it be?" Only when I choose the former do I find myself enjoying who He has created me to be. The rest of the time, I'm striving and pushing, loathing the poor decision I made and wondering why I am struggling so much. One springs from a place of trust; the other comes from a place of severe distrust and pride to believe that I have all the power I need without God.

When we look down at the wounds we have suffered in this life, we quickly realize this is not what we want. We didn't ask for any of this, to be disappointed and disillusioned regarding the heart of God, the Father. And we realize that this wasn't what God intended. You see, that elusive sweet spot that the world writes about and desires more than anything is played out in the relationship between Jesus and God. When we see how Jesus lived and related to God while on earth, it's what we really want. It almost feels like playing. And when we capture it ourselves, it's like we get this internal giggle that springs from an understanding that we're loved and that our Father is going to take care of us.

We stop striving to create and succeed on our own power, turn instead to our Father and ask, "What's next? What do you want me to do?" Suddenly, life isn't about our agenda and our plan, but it's about what God wants us to do, all the while knowing that He will provide all the resources and wisdom we need to do it.

Jesus was always working one person at a time, followed by this simple question: "Who's next?" It wasn't about changing the world with one big meeting, but about starting a powerful revolution one heart at a time. As we look intently at Jesus' life, we see his Father's smile reflected over His life. He operated just like He saw God operating, caring deeply and intimately about each person as an individual. And that's how we can live, too, once our wound is healed by understanding that God's love for us is unconditional.

When we experience God's blessing over our lives—not a "blessing" of material possessions but of simple approval and affirmation that He loves us because of who we are; when we discover how to catch God's smile over our lives; when we learn to live under God's smile; when we learn to pass God's smile on to others—that's when we experience the power of His unconditional love and acceptance in our lives.

CHAPTER THREE

The Way of the Smile

For Jews in Jesus' day, it was difficult to understand who God, the Father, was. They saw their salvation coming not from a person, but from their ability to keep the law, the Sabbath, and the land that had been promised to them. When this Galilean prophet started healing the sick, casting out demons and raising the dead, His message created a revolution everywhere He went. And when Jesus started teaching that God was Father, Abba, it sent shockwaves, challenging everything they believed about God.

Isaiah talked about the way Jesus would be when he wrote this scripture:

He will not crush those who are weak or quench the smallest hope. He will bring full justice to all who have been wronged. (Isaiah 42:3, NLT)

The way of God's smile on earth wasn't pushy; it gave life. Jesus had room in His heart for those who never were invited to the parties of the religious elite. Jesus broke down the class system by making healing and love available to anyone who was hungry. This was a new way of thinking for a group of people who staked their hope in a deliverer who would set them free from the bondage of Roman oppression. Jesus' way was not what they expected from the Messiah. However, Jesus wasn't trying to pander to the crowd; He was living under the smile of His Father, relishing God's blessing and unconditional love that was being showered down upon Him from heaven.

When you're living under the smile of the Father, you know it. It's unmatched in the confidence it gives you to be yourself, to be who God has created you to be. You sense the joy He has over your life. From a practical standpoint, it feels like you've just been handed a blank check to go pursue your dreams. Naysayers, doubt, lack of experience or skills—they all become collectively muted as your faith grows. You begin to experience what it's like to simply be under the smile of the father. And anything you get to do feels like playing. It's "the way" Jesus talked about when He said, "I am the way, the truth, and the life." His way was to bask in the smile of His Father and enjoy the great adventure before Him. Jesus didn't have to strive for His Father's love—He knew He had it.

As I've experienced this in my own life, one of my favorite things is to watch other people catch God's smile over their lives. With great anticipation I await the "ah-h a " moment when the lights come on—both inside and out.

Tears and Tiaras

I was recently invited to perform a rites of passage ceremony for the Walter Hoving Home, a faith-based rehabilitation center located in Pasadena, Calif., for women involved in prostitution, drugs, alcohol and abusive situations. These women have been devastated, suffering severe abuse and mistreatment by people in all walks of life. And they enter the home completely broken, tired of running and trying to put their lives back together on their own.

When I arrived at the home, this group of women was nearing the end of the program. While living there, they learned a whole new way of life through reading the Bible, praying and seeking God. For almost a year, they were nurtured by gracious leaders whose life passion was to restore what had been taken from these young women.

As I stood before these ladies, I began sharing the message about the difference the Father in Heaven could make in their lives. The tears started flowing as the loving presence of Jesus filled that room, touching each one in just the right place where they had been robbed and devastated. One woman I met didn't have many teeth left in her mouth; she was beaten, abused, neglected, and became enslaved to a life of drug addiction. She was nearly toothless because she ended up pulling out most of her teeth with pliers one night in a drug-induced tirade. As she stood before me, it was evident that something had changed in her that day. Something had given her hope.

As I listened to some of their stories, many were the same: Their father wasn't there for them. "My dad was in prison" or "My dad was there but never really present" were some of their typical responses. But this should come as no surprise. In Paul Vitz's book, *Faith of the Fatherless*, his research among famous atheists finds that most of them either had absent or abusive fathers—and they hated their dads for it. Not having the voice of a father in our lives makes us angry and discontent. We lash out in one way or another at the world, upset that we were somehow cheated by the natural order God intended. It leads us down treacherous paths in life, either one that leads to our external destruction or one that eats us alive from the inside. And these women were the result of both. Sure, many had heard the message of a heavenly Father who loved them, but it wasn't surprising they were never able to connect with His love for them as individuals.

After I finished sharing, we began our rites of passage ceremony, a moment where we would usher in this blessing over their lives and they might experience God's smile over their lives for the first time. I stood at the top of this beautiful walnut staircase that wound up through the center of the mansion that had been turned into a home for God's princesses. My cousin Jeanne, who had arranged this event with some of her friends, passed out warm hugs and sparkling tiaras to each of the women. As I called out these women one by one, Jeanne and her friends slipped the tiaras on the women's heads. Then we all applauded, cheered and wept as we watched each hurt little girl in a woman's body walk down that staircase and away from the life that had been stolen from by abuse and into a life blessed by God.

To say it was awesome would be an understatement. What broke my heart that day was the knowledge that I might be the first man in their lives who wasn't coming with selfish intentions, to take something from them. But rather, I was coming to give them something—the blessing of God the Father—and to release them into the healthy adult womanhood that was their destiny under Christ.

Just when we thought we had wiped away the last tear, the women who had come with my cousin to minister to the women in the home stepped toward me. They weren't slaves to drugs or alcohol or prostitution; they came from influential families in Southern California. They had little social or economic similarities to the women living in the Walter Hoving Home.

The first volunteer broke the ice. "My dad never blessed me either," she admitted. Before I could say anything, one of the women who had just been given a tiara, gave hers back to the woman and said, "Why don't you take mine?" She walked to the top of the stairs toward me and said to me with tears in her eyes, "I want what my dad didn't or couldn't give me, too." One by one, this women's ministry team received the unconditional love and acceptance of Jesus' Father. All they ever wanted from their own fathers was love and acceptance, but their fathers were performance driven because of their own unhealed wounds. Consequently, they were not equipped to bless their daughters whole heartedly.

But that day, women from vastly different ends of the life spectrum came together and shared a common experience—the love and pleasure of their Father in Heaven. In one life-changing moment, they began to understand "the way." This is "the way" we are called to live, to know the unconditional love and acceptance of God and to bask in His blessing. And this is the way Jesus lived. Just exactly how did Jesus live in this joy?

Who is Your Audience?

Can you imagine a life where your circumstances don't determine how you see yourself? While Jesus suffered more discouragement and persecution in three years of ministry than most of us will experience in a lifetime, He also lived in the confidence that the voice backing Him up had all of the resources of heaven to help Him accomplish the assignment He was given each day. Jesus didn't run in desperation from town to town or push His way into a meeting. He could speak a brilliant sermon and then disappear into a crowd in a moment. And in three short years of public ministry, He changed the world. Calendars are set by His birth. If you read closely, you'll never find Jesus asking, "How am I doing, Father?" He never seemed lost in His journey, despite the crumbling circumstances around Him.

One of the things I noticed about Jesus is that who He was as a person came from the way He served those around Him. He felt secure enough in Himself that He didn't need to show off; in fact, He often needled the religious leaders of the day because of the freedom and joy He lived under. He was devoid of the pressure to perform.

Remember the question that my friend asked me: "Who is in your audience?" Who did you come up with? Who you see around your table determines how you live your life. Jesus made this statement: "I only do what I see my Father doing." Think of the trust in that statement. Or consider the wisdom in this one: "I only speak what I hear my Father saying." Before He left, Jesus promised that we would do even greater things than He did. He not only talked about this but He lived it. The effectiveness of my life as a leader, a father, or a husband is directly proportional to the singleness of the audience for which I'm playing. Jesus learned that the audience of One was the secret of a fulfilling life.

In his book *The Relentless Tenderness of Jesus*, Brennan Manning writes:

> "Living out of the center frees us from the tyranny of peer pressure. Living to please the Father, as Jesus did, becomes the basic impulse of a Christian's life—more important than pleasing people. And this requires a remarkable degree of freedom. Jesus was not intimidated by public opinion, by what 'others will think.' In order to be free for the outcasts, the sinners, the marginals in His social world, Jesus had to keep His distance from the expectations and the moralizing judgments of the authorities and the respectable. ... He was going to the home of Zacchaeus because this sinner was a child of His Father, that was all. And that's the name of that tune."

God's heart is for us, the people in this world. And the things that were important to the Father became important to the Son. Jesus enjoyed people, so much so that it marked His life. Jesus had this pervasive smile on His face. There was joy in His life because of whose Son He was, not because of anything He had accomplished in His own power.

As soon as we earn a victory in our lives, we wear it as a badge of honor and hit everyone on the head who doesn't honor it. But Jesus wasn't like that—and He was the Son of God. He could have dinner with a Pharisee and the next night hang around some people who believed that drunkenness was the way to live.

Jesus was irresistible because of the way He lived and for whom He lived, ultimately giving Himself away in every encounter to the person who was in front of Him. Not feeling the need to push and take, He blessed. He encouraged. He modeled a life that lived under the smile of God.

Once, as Jesus doodled in the dirt, the Pharisees forced the issue with Him again. A woman caught in the act of adultery was thrust before Jesus. Intending to trap Jesus, the Pharisees wanted to know what should be done; they wanted His approval to stone her like Moses' law taught or watch Him rebel against the law in front of a crowd. The moment was tense for Jesus' detractors, but He didn't even look up. With rocks still in the Pharisees and angry mob's

hands, Jesus words dispelled the allusion of self-righteous-
ness: "If any one of you is without sin, let him be the first
to throw a stone at her" (John 8:7, NIV). Surely bracing for
a life-ending deluge of hurled rocks, the woman had to be
stunned at her moment of redemption. Her picture of God
had to be turned upside down, for He wasn't an angry God
ready to condemn, but a tender God, quick to love.

What's even more extraordinary is Jesus' question
after the crowd dispersed: "Where are your accusers?" In an
instant, that question dispelled the fear in her. Jesus, who
being God Himself, said, "Neither do I accuse you." He
broke the power of accusation upon her and gave her a
blessing: "Go and sin no more." Notice Jesus didn't say,
"You've got to live up to the rules now if you want My
love." He said, "From this moment on because of who I
am, these words that I now speak to you will change you
forever. You're going to live from My blessing and not be
the object of other men's lust." Jesus broke the curse over
this woman who had been robbed of joy by men her entire
life. Heaven was smiling upon her—and she had to feel it.

That's what awaits you amidst your pain and brokenness. There is nothing in life sweeter than watching the
power of God's blessing descend upon broken lives and
transform them forever.

CHAPTER FOUR

Catching God's Smile

Through my travels I meet men and women like me who lost their fathers early in their life. There is a special place in God's heart for those of us who have lost our fathers on earth. We are not only called to receive the love of Jesus in our lives, but also the Father's love. It takes courage to bring your brokenness to Him and let His loving arms lead you home. It is easier for some to stay mad at God than to face the pain of our past. I have watched some in our conferences hold back because the wound between them and their father was too painful.

One day while praying about the pain of losing my dad and the life I have tried to build from the wreckage of that plane, God spoke to my heart and said, "The last word your father heard was 'come', and I have called you to call people to come to Me." My heart was overwhelmed as I could see the arms of Jesus catch my father at 400 miles an hour. I realized that if you get Jesus, you also get His Father too. God spoke into the biggest question mark in my life and filled it with the His unconditional love and acceptance. My heavenly Father's unconditional love for me has touched me in the deepest place in my heart. My challenge, like yours, is to push away from the things we use to make ourselves known, in order to pull towards Jesus and His Father.

Made to be Celebrated

Did you know that you were made by God to be seen and noticed? There is something deep inside of us that yearns for affirmation for what we have done.

Recently I finished a wood project in my garage; the project left me covered from head to toe in wood glue and sawdust. Ready to show off my masterpiece, I called Jill to the garage. "Hey, honey, come and look!" I shouted, proud of my finished product. My wife is so gracious when it comes to my projects. Her response is usually something like, "Wow, honey! You are amazing! What is it?" We all want affirmation from others.

Some people might say, "Well, Ed, I never do anything to be seen here on earth. I only do things for heaven." That is a noble sentiment, but God still made us human. I just hand those people my hand sewn superman costume and tell them to go for it. There is nothing wrong with human affirmation; however, we must guard against it becoming our life's quest.

We were designed by God to have a relationship with Him and to be celebrated by Him. Consequently, there is something inside of us that yearns to be noticed and celebrated and seen by our earthly fathers, too. Even though moms faithfully show up at every Little League game, kids are always looking for their dads. Joshua, my youngest champion-to-be, puffs out his little chest as soon as I show up. He is always looking at my face for the affirmation he needs to swing for the fence. God has made me as a father to be the first audience for my children, and when I am there for them, I communicate the deeper truth that God will always be there for them, too. My applause can help my kids hear the audience of the One for whom we have been designed.

Screen diva Marlene Dietrich so missed her past cabaret ovations that she even issued recordings—two sides of nothing but applause. Her biographer writes that she would invite her friends Judy Garland and Noel Coward over to listen to them and insisted on playing both sides. "That was Rio," she told them. "That was Cologne. That was Chicago." She was hungry for the heart of God but was duped into thinking that human applause was enough to satisfy her taste.

Whose applause do you hear? What do you really think God thinks about you? Is He disappointed? Are you disappointed with where you are today?

Authenticity in Our Relationship with God

One day while taking a walk on the beach, I spotted two silvery objects delicately embedded in the sand. One was a nickel, a genuine five-cent piece of U.S. currency. The other was a plastic nickel, which did its best to look like a real nickel with the exception of the small notation on it stating it was not valid as currency.

For most of us, the plastic nickel represents our lives. We so desperately want to be real and authentic. But instead of becoming a real nickel, we spend our lives trying to look like one. We go to great efforts and extremes to emulate everything about it—the texture, the weight, the markings. In the end, it's not worth the five cents it represents. So, instead of asking how to look like a real nickel, we must begin asking how we can become a real nickel. How do our lives move from this current reality of fallacy and brokenness to a future reality of authenticity and wholeness?

The answer comes when we catch God's smile over

our lives. Realizing that He loves us simply because we are His, we lay down all our striving and feel God's pleasure over our lives. It's like the difference between two kids spending time with their fathers. One begs an answer of the question, "What do you think, dad?"; the other runs into his playful father's arms and says, "Do it again, daddy!"

The second child has caught his father's smile over his life. He's not trying to perform. He's not seeking approval. He's not trying to prove himself. He merely understands his father loves him—and nothing will change that. Unaware of his dad's sore arms and aching back from playing this same game for the past hour, he will beg his dad to throw him in the air one more time. We need to move to this place of enjoying and basking in God's approval.

The Apostle John's writings show that he caught God's smile over his life. His work and life reflect the courage that results from a deep knowledge of oneself and of one's position with God. He wrote of the power of a relationship laid bare. Consider his words on our relationship with God:

We proclaim to you what we have seen and heard, so that you also may have fellowship with us. And our fellowship is with the Father and with his Son, Jesus Christ. We write this to make our joy complete. (1 John 1:3-4, NIV)

Take a moment to ponder what this word means to you: *fellowship*. What does it represent? What images come to mind? What does fellowship with God mean?

In current terms, fellowship simply implies "hanging out" together. When I think of just getting together and "hanging out" with someone, I think of sharing my time and attention with someone I care about. We may laugh together, cry together, pray together, or swap stories with each other. With a true friend, I feel no pressure to perform.

If I'm in true fellowship with you, I don't have to put on my "pastor hat" or my "former NFL lineman hat." I don't have to put on my "expert hat" or "writer hat." I just get to be me, while inviting you to be who God made you to be—without pretense or self-consciousness. In that moment I'm not worried or hyper-vigilant about whether you'll enjoy me for who I am or who I am not. I am so confident in our relationship that I know you'll enjoy who I am—just as I know that I will enjoy who you are. We have ceased being plastic nickels.

I wish I could tell you that I have always stayed in a place of being authentic. I have deposited many plastic nickels into relationships around me, instead of giving them the real me. Those times of name dropping, telling only my best stories, and always presenting my best side have worn out my nickel-making machine. This is what makes us look fake and religious to the world. A friend of mine says religion begins in you the moment you start making lists, the moment you start comparing yourself to others, the moment superiority hits your heart. It's difficult to feel superior and have compassion at the same time.

Jesus had the answer for the shallowness that we all have felt. He shared His Father's captured heart with us. His relationship through His Father's smile opened a new kind of life for us to experience. But this life wasn't free. The Father allowed His only Son to be sacrificed so that we could experience the joy of relationship. Instead of feeling like we must live from a place of eternal striving, God says, "Come to Me, all who are weary. Rest in My love. Drink from the fountains of My table. Experience relationship with Me." The only way to live this life is through being forgiven. Only total forgiveness can set a striving heart free; without forgiveness we continually try to make up for the bad that we do, and that is an endless cycle.

Are you looking for a new way to do life? Forget trying to look good for God—Jesus just wants to hang out with you and introduce you to His Dad. .

How Jesus Caught God's Smile

In *The Difference a Father Makes*, I discussed how the

Father made explicit to Jesus, in His baptism by John the Baptist, how He really felt about Jesus. This was a defining moment in Jesus' life. After being baptized, as Jesus came out of the water, the heavens were opened and He saw the Spirit of God descending as a dove and lighting on Him, and a voice out of the heavens said, "This is My beloved Son, in whom I am well-pleased."

This was not a statement made by God near the end of Jesus' time on earth when we would probably shrug our shoulders and say, "Well, of course, Jesus deserves some acknowledgment. Look at all He did." This statement—this demonstration—of His love for Jesus was made before He performed His first miracle. In practical terms, Jesus hadn't yet done a thing. God was not giving Jesus an "atta boy" because He had performed well by healing the lame or the lepers, or turned a few fish and loaves into a meal for thousands. There had been no miracles, no words of wisdom, no appreciable effort whatsoever. This was Jesus, the simple carpenter; all He had done up until that point was handcraft tables and chairs. Was that really deserving of God's ringing endorsement?

Well, if you live in a performance-based mindset, it wasn't. But if you understand that God's heart is for relationship, and that nothing Jesus ever did could make the Father love Him any more or any less, then it begins to make sense. They were in relationship with one another; God was crazy about His Son. He was smiling over Jesus' life not because of anything He did, but because of who He was. And the feelings were mutual. Jesus modeled a life based on the complete, unquestioning acceptance of His Father. He and His father were one. (John 10:30) They were in seamless communication.

We cannot earn God's smile. In your life, you can compile lists of great achievements—and God will smile over you with the same love and tenderness as He does a child dying of AIDS in Africa. You can be the President of the United States and God will smile over your life just as much as He will over a school custodian.

Once this reality hits home for us, we cease all our plotting, striving, and scheming—and we learn to release ourselves to trust God fully just as we are. We get on with the joy of living and leave behind the business of making positive impressions.

Remembering the Smile

Maybe you've experienced God's smile over your life before, but through the everyday humdrum of life you've forgotten about it. The voices within this world become so loud that they drown out the tender voice of the Father speaking His love to you. As a result, it's easy for you to wrestle with the insecurity of your flesh.

Why do we run and hide like Adam and Eve in the Garden of Eden when we feel shame? Shouldn't God be the first one we turn to for help? But it's a universal response—our first instinct when ashamed or embarrassed is to hide and immediately do something that minimizes our sense of inadequacy. It's no wonder we react that way. It's almost instinctual—and then it's reinforced through the misinterpretation of Scripture. Take this passage in John, for instance:

"I am the true vine, and My Father is the vinedresser. Every branch in Me that does not bear fruit, He takes away; and every branch that bears fruit, He prunes it so that it may bear more fruit. (John 15:1-2, NASB)

Some members of my family own a vineyard in northern California, and I've spent some time there trying to learn more about the process. What I have discovered made me return to the Scripture and look a little closer at the meaning of this particular passage. Let me give you a picture of what it's like to be a vinedresser, which I believe will bring more clarity to the above passage and be more in line with the heart of God. The vinedresser tends the vine so that it may produce more fruit—productivity is priority number one. After the harvest when all the grapes and shoots are gathered, the vinedresser takes the most fruitful branches and prunes them back near the top of the vine so it will be a fruit bearing vine the following year.

But here is where what a vinedresser does departs with this interpretation of the text. Though there are branches that aren't producing fruit, the vinedresser knows they all have fruit-bearing potential. There is a major reason they don't produce—the branch has fallen off the trellis that holds up the vine. A branch cannot produce fruit if it's lying on the ground. It's damp, gathering mold, hidden from the sun and unable to get the light it needs. It's completely disconnected from the rest of the branches.

The vinedresser doesn't cut off these branches. Instead, the vinedresser will collect these branches and gently place them back on the trellis so they may produce fruit again. The Greek word translated "takes away" is more accurately translated "lifts up." It's a more realistic image of what's occurring in the vineyard as vinedressers search the vineyard for fallen branches, not in an attempt to remove them, but rather, to reconnect them to the vine.

When we fall on the ground, we become broken, bruised and disconnected. We lose the light and sustenance we need. We are cut off from our life-giving source, and we stop producing fruit. When we struggle to see God's smile over our lives during these times, we mistakenly make the assumption that God is stalking the vineyard, looking for the next branch to whack—and assume it's going to be us.

That's why we run. That's why Adam and Eve ran. That overwhelming sense of shame at the sight of our own sin and inconsistency compels us to hide. We think God will never want to have anything to do with us. That's how the enemy operates. First, he entices us to sin and then he makes us feel shameful for doing so.

But God is not looking for a branch to whack—He is looking for one to raise up, to lift back onto the trellis and reconnect to the vine. He is rooting for us, cheering us on, waiting for us at the finish line with wide-open arms. He gently lifts our branch out of the moldy water, cleans us off, and beams with joy as we begin to come alive again.

That's the redemptive heart of God that shines on us when we're broken. God's smile over our lives doesn't go away, even when we've fallen short. He's still there, smiling in the same warm way He was the first time you saw Him.

The Object, Not the Subject

In 1963 Sherwood E. Wirt interviewed C.S. Lewis and asked him this question: "Do you feel that you made a decision at the time of your conversion?"

"I would not put it that way. What I wrote in *Surprised by Joy* was that 'before God closed in on me, I was offered what now appears a moment of wholly free choice.' But I feel my decision was not so important. I was the object rather than the subject in this affair. I was decided upon. I was glad afterwards at the way it came out, but at the moment what I heard was God saying, 'Put down your gun and we'll talk.'"

That is what it means to be caught by His smile. I loved the way C.S. Lewis put it: "I was the object rather than the subject in this affair."

It was the same thing for me. When Jesus' loving gaze captured my heart, it was not that I had come to a new moral enlightenment; rather, it was that the audience of my life that had changed. I knew in a moment that I had always been the object of the love of God. But in the moment of my yielding to allow myself to be loved, love itself captured my heart. It was the gaze of my Father in Heaven through the eyes of Jesus that met me on a hospital gurney while faced with a possible career-ending surgery.

I knew inside the deepest part of me that His smile over me was not because of my own attempts to prove myself. It came because I was His beloved. Just like His Son. The gaze that led Jesus to fulfill His purpose was there for me as well. From that point forward, becoming the receiver of the pleasure of God has been my quest, my new goal line for living.

Whether He is opening blind eyes or touching broken hearts, our Father in Heaven is good and wants us to know the same creative life that His Son lived on earth. Receiving the power of God's blessing over our lives offers us the opportunity of a life filled with love and connection. The experience of God's smile over our lives sets us free from the endless pursuit of trying to prove ourselves to obtain the love we hunger for so deeply. That's the life that Jesus lived. That's the way, the truth and the life He came to bring us.

CHAPTER FIVE

Living Under God's Smile

While the idea of having God smiling over our lives sounds wonderful, what does this look like for us? How do we live under God's smile day in and day out? Like most people, I found it difficult to connect to the idea of God smiling over me just because we had a relationship. So, through the years, I made many attempts to cajole a smile out of God for something I did. One of the most memorable episodes occurred with my first attempt to fulfill the calling on my life.

Lobsters for Jesus?

When God stirred my heart to enter into full-time ministry, the first question that came to mind was, "How am I going to pay for this?" After seeing the haunting images of televangelists begging for money, I shuddered thinking about myself in that role. I wanted to figure out a way to earn enough money to fund my ministry. In reality, what was behind all my scheming was sheer terror. I had the physical skill to be a pro athlete—now I was moving into uncharted waters. And I was terrified.

So, I sought godly counsel in the form of a man who told me his grand story about how much money I could make as a lobster fisherman. I then took all my money, bought a boat and headed to Catalina Island to make the fortune that would fund my endeavors. Little did I know that *el niño* would be so severe that year that it would devastate the lobster industry around the island.

One evening while I was out on my boat, a big storm had blown in and my lobster pots were being crushed against the cliffs by the waves. After eight hours of bone crushing work, I saw three lobster pots tangled together near the cliffs in shallow water. I desperately tried to grab them with a hook to put them on my wench and pull them up before a large wave could toss me into the treacherous rocks. However, in my tired and frantic state, I didn't notice the line drifting beneath my motor. Before I knew it, the motor choked down as the line wrapped around the propeller.

Suddenly, I was anchored to the bottom with only one

difficult way to escape. Fear had driven me to this place because I didn't trust God would take care of me. Years later, I learned that *living under God's smile is about trusting and risking in the One who is always there and always generous.*

What happened next seemed like it took forever but probably lasted mere seconds. I felt like the Lord very clearly said to me, "Preach or drown." In this instance, I realized I had run from the love and protection of God's calling and put myself in harm's way. My fear of having to trust God for the provision of my family, instead of my own ability to predict and determine my life, had driven me away from His smile.

I shouted to the heavens, "OK, I will preach the Gospel and go anywhere You send me, if You save me from this." I restarted my engines and gunned it. The ropes that anchored the boat broke. As I turned, a huge wave threatened to engulf "The Narcosis." I was barely able to power the boat over the top of it because the propeller was still choked with the line.

I motored beyond where the waves were peaking, grabbed a fishing knife, and jumped into the water to try and chop the rope off the propeller so I could motor back to port. (Have you ever tried to swim and repent at the same time? Trust me, it's not easy.) I wasn't able to time the boat's lurching up and down, so I grabbed the coiled rope that was around the propeller. A mis-timed swing with my knife gashed my left hand. Blood started pumping out of my hand and the *Jaws* theme song started playing in my head. Every wave looked like a shark's fin and immediately I felt like I could relate to Jonah. "Help me, God! I don't want to die like this!" I yelled.

I composed myself enough to attempt another swing with my knife. After a brief struggle, I managed to cut the rope free from the motor. However, in my haste when I jumped off the side of the boat, I forgot that the swim plank was tied to the rusty lobster pots on the back of the boat. My climb back into the boat wouldn't be easy. In the process, the pots' jagged edges shredded my chest. Convinced I was going to die of some ghastly infection, I grabbed rubbing alcohol and poured it all over my chest.

Still alive, I motored around to the backside of the harbor and docked my boat. All I could think about was getting to a phone and calling my wife to let her know that I was a) alive and b) finished with this lobster fishing gig.

I called Jill and told her I was repenting. She told me to come home right away. On my return trip home, I felt like a broken stick or an empty branch. There was no fruit on my tree. I had spent thousands of dollars trying to build a new business and no fruit had come of it because my efforts had taken root in fear, not under the smile of the

Father. When I got home, I sat on the couch with my first-born in my lap and said, "OK, Lord. I'm in the ministry."

That was a big moment in my life. I write about it with laughter now, but it wasn't remotely humorous at the time. Have you ever had those moments of sheer terror where you feel like you're called to do something and you have no resources to do it? You're afraid to try so you attempt to control the situation, or you live with reckless abandon, making dumb choices while presuming God will supply the resources. Fear drove me to throw myself off my own bridge. But there is a better way.

No More Pushing

When you live in a place of understanding God's acceptance of who you are, you are drawn into the destiny for which He has called you instead of feeling the need to push your way in.

John of the Cross, the 16th Century Spanish mystic, wrote about how we move from a state of depravity to fully understanding God's love for us in his timeless classic, *The Dark Night of the Soul*. He writes,

"But now that the soul has put on its other and working attire—that of aridity and abandonment—

and now that its first lights have turned into darkness, it possesses these lights more truly in this virtue of self-knowledge, which is so excellent and so necessary, considering itself now as nothing and experiencing no satisfaction in itself; for it sees that it does nothing of itself neither can do anything."

Trying to be a lobster fisherman was my dark night of the soul. I wanted to do what God wanted me to do—but I wanted to do it my way. I thought maybe He would be proud of me and my plan; rather, He was simply waiting for me to trust Him and experience His love and mercy in ways I had never known.

Jesus said, "I am the vine; you are the branches. If a man remains in me and I in him, he will bear much fruit; apart from me you can do nothing" (John 15:5, NIV). The life that God has called us to live happens when we hear that voice that says, "You are my beloved." It's the same voice that served as a compass to Jesus when He walked out in His journey. We need to remain in Him, not because God is a control freak, but because He loves us and wants to show us His amazing love that results in a trusting relationship, one that is not based upon anything else. When we are connected with the living God, we get permission to move from performance to a place of trust in His grace.

Finding His Smile Everyday

Moving from catching God's smile over our lives to living under it happens when we understand the power in relationship with Him. We transition from trying to plot out some epic Christian journey to simply living it daily as we follow God's voice in our lives and respond with a heart full of trust and dependence upon Him. God isn't trying to lead us down some perilous path; on the contrary, He is trying to show us His love for us and help us catch His heart for others.

This transition began in my own heart when I began to study intently how Jesus lived His life. He trusted His Father every step of the way. But I also saw it in someone who is easier for me to relate to—King David. We can all probably relate more to a guy who has made numerous mistakes than we can to the perfect Son of God. Over and over in David's life, we find that he came back to the one thing that was his only source of life—his relationship with God.

The blessing of the Father opens the doorway to relationship with Him. But when we start living under His Smile, we catch His joy over our lives every day.

Part of that connection for me is having that childlike, everyday walk with Him, first connecting with Him in private so I can see Him work in public.

Where Are You Rooted?

Have you ever driven through a desert and seen a stream? When our family drives to Mammoth Mountain for vacation we notice these little springs in the middle of the desert; they feed the biggest oak trees you can imagine. The trees remain green because they are rooted in life-giving water.

Then there are tumbleweeds, rolling balls of dead and dried up twigs and leaves. They are lifeless, despite their seemingly boundless energy in being blown from one disparate part of the desert to the next. Where you are rooted determines your fruitfulness. Tumbleweeds are created when the spring rains fall in the desert. Their roots are turned up because they are born during the rains. When the rains stop, their roots lose their footing and they are easily uprooted by the wind. Hence, they become tumbleweeds.

Are you rooted by a stream of living water, confident in who God has called you to be and enjoying the journey set before you? Or are you tumbling from one hobby to the next, one relationship to the next, one marriage to the next, one adrenaline rush to the next, searching for … something … if you only knew what?

Jeremiah is a great example in Scripture of a young man who understands how to finish his race. He was called to be a prophet as a teenager and had to face the discouragement of not having one of his prophetic words listened to by Israel. How did he survive the discouragement that woke him up everyday?

"This is what the Lord says: 'Cursed is the one who trusts in man, who depends on flesh for his strength and whose heart turns away from the Lord. He will be like a bush in the wastelands; he will not see prosperity when it comes. He will dwell in the parched places of the desert, in a salt land where no one lives.' But blessed is the man who trusts in the Lord, whose confidence is in him. He will be like a tree planted by the water that sends out its roots by the stream. It does not fear when heat comes; its leaves are always green. It has no worries in a year of drought and never fails to bear fruit." (Jeremiah 17:5-8, NIV)

Jeremiah learned how to dig down into the stream of the Lord. His hard times drove him back to God, and more than 2,000 years later His prophetic words are still being listened to and preached from the rooftops. The fruitfulness of a life that lives in the favor of God extends beyond our 70-something years and blossoms into eternity.

When you get this understanding, you will begin to taste the joy Jesus experienced. Your circumstances will not determine the smile on your face. That is why the Bible says,

"The joy of the Lord is your strength." (Nehemiah 8:10, NIV) It is supernatural because it flows out of the depth of being loved unconditionally by the Father and His Son. It will flow out of your entire existence.

Who's That Smiling Teacher?

When people compared the current teachers of the day, there was one who stood above the pettiness of religion; He had no problem going to party at Matthew's house, being touched by an unclean woman, or being associated with a bunch of unsuccessful fishermen. He seemed unaffected by the cheers and the jeers of the crowds. He had a relationship with His Father that was a magnet to the fatherless and the socially dispossessed.

This understanding of His relationship with God is why Jesus was so attractive to those around Him, yet such an irritant to the religious leaders of His day. He knew who He was and what He was here for. He was the first totally centered man, and that was irresistible to those tired of their own attempts of trying to be religiously presentable to a God whose love they never felt. Jesus didn't come to win a popularity contest; He came to serve as a sacrifice so that every man, woman and child could know what it means to enter into relationship with God the Father.

Jesus was able to be the smiling teacher because He smiled on the inside. He was tender with others because He was tender with Himself. Compassion flows from understanding that you are totally loved and liked by God. Learning to live from the grace on God's face will transform how you see yourself and how you treat others. It is almost impossible to love others when your heart is filled with disdain for yourself.

Let me explain. There was a time years ago when I had just finished chewing out my oldest son Edward for his poor performance. I had just broken one of my own cardinal rules: I would be loving and not brutal to my kids.

Totally disgusted with myself because I had crushed my 11-year-old son, I walked into my office and cried out to the Lord, "Why do I do that?" The Lord interrupted my despair and answered me, "Ed, that is the way you talk to yourself." His words stopped me in my tracks. "Ed, you learned to hear My voice through the filter of the harsh words you heard from your step-father, coaches and mentors in your life. When you learn how to hear My voice and come to know what I really think about you, it will change the way you talk to yourself and the way you relate to your kids and others."

Learning to experience our relationship with God like that changes our heart toward ourselves and others. If you could hear the loud and angry rebukes that have been internalized, you would understand how those silent voices still drown out the tenderness for which you have been created.

Being and feeling completely loved negates our preoccupation with ourselves. And it is at that moment that our inverted eyes are opened to see what Jesus saw and how He walked around looking for what His Father was up to. Because Jesus was so preoccupied with others, He was free to give himself to those God brought His way. Doesn't that sound like a free life to you? That is the place where God's kingdom comes and miracles happen before your eyes.

Jesus was tender toward those who came up and interrupted His day because He was tenderized by His relationship with His Father. His grasp of that rich truth translates into a powerful lesson for us today: If we spend time with God each day, we don't have to pray for a time to do ministry. He will show us His heart and what He wants us to do wherever we are in life, whatever we are doing. And then it's about courageously releasing ourselves into those Father smiling moments.

He has blessed us so that we can become a blessing. Every gift that we have needs someone with whom to share it or else it is meaningless. Living under His smile is not just about us—it's about being His hands and feet to those who desperately need to experience God's love through us.

CHAPTER SIX

Passing It On

Whether it is with your family, friends, or strangers on the street, showing others how much God loves them just because they are human is guaranteed to turn your world—and the lives of others—upside down. The power of approval and acceptance speaks to one of our deepest needs. Everyone wants to be approved in some form or fashion. We all want to know that our lives count, that we matter to someone else.

I recently received this letter from a dad who not only caught God's smile over his life but was intent on passing it along to his children:

"Since my son was at college, I drove to see him three and a half hours away. We watched the playoff games, then went out to eat and finally out on a walk around the university. God gave me the perfect time to tell him how proud I am of him and what specifically I liked about him. And then I told him that I feel he has become a man in my eyes and that no longer will I treat him as a child.

"He was stunned and silent, but I could tell immediately how good he felt and how powerful that statement was to him. We hugged each other with the best hug I have ever had from him and probably the best hug he'd had from me.

"The next day he called his sister and told her it was the best time he had ever had with his Dad. I can't wait to see how our relationship grows in the years ahead and how he grows as a man."

That story captures the heart of God for us. God rejoices over us with singing and dances over us with joy. It's His heart that's ever waiting, ever wanting to bless and give life to others. This is what Jesus came to bring us—and that is our mission: to catch God's heart and give it away.

Your approval will become evident when you begin to see the beauty of your daughters and you're able to communicate that in real time. Or you're able to look in your son's direction—whether he has a heat gun in his hand or has just made the winning basket in the championship game—and you can celebrate those moments that enable him to understand that no matter what he does, he never has to work for the smile of his mom or dad again. Imagine a life lived out of that kind of confidence. That life becomes reality as people—kids, friends, anyone—begin to embrace God's love and acceptance in their lives.

Helping Your Kids Embrace God's Love

One question people ask me all the time is this: How do you build structure around your kids' dreams? In other words, what parents really want to know is how they can help their children come to such a place in life that they know they are unconditionally loved and feel free to pursue whatever God has placed on their hearts to do. When your kids not only hear that from you, but also feel it and know it's true, get ready! They are about to blossom into a world-changing force.

As a parent, you have to refrain from projecting your dreams onto your kids' lives and allow them to discover what it is that God has planted inside them. Part of helping your kids understand what it means to embrace God's love and acceptance for their lives is by modeling for them the way God treats you. In the way He communicates with you, in the way He uses His voice, in the way He uses His power—you must avoid compartmentalizing. God never uses His presence to push anyone around, and neither should you. When you model God's love for your kids, they see your heart. In my desire to help my kids embrace God's love, I have to check my heart and make sure that I'm in line with what God desires for them.

Recently, my son Luke began wrestling with the decision of whether or not to continue playing football. I told him it was his decision to make. So, he went out for the team and made it, setting himself up to be one of the top three players on the team. Then I asked him what he was going to do.

"What's your decision?" I asked.

"Dad, will you still like me if I don't play football this year?" he responded.

"I have a question for you: Do you think I won't? Do you feel as though football is your destiny?" I responded (For years, many people have compared Luke's athletic ability to mine, yet his heart is captured by worship and serving the Lord).

He said, "No, Dad, I know you'll back me up in whatever I do." He was just checking in with me. Our children are always watching our looks and listening to our tone.

Are you serving the dreams that originate inside your children, or are you driving them toward something you think is good for them?

I wish I could tell you that this was easy for me to do. Being a highly competitive man, it is easy to fall back into the routine of driving my kids instead of equipping them to handle the wheel. The only solution for this would-be smile chaser is my own commitment to nurturing my heart by spending time with my Father each day. I have learned that I can only give away the smile I catch for myself.

While Luke was watching me help his brother pursue a professional golf career, he was wondering, *Dad, do you really believe the words you write and preach?* Part of enabling my kids to see my unconditional love for them requires me to live in a present way, ensuring that I spend time with them and commit to building my relationship with them. Remember dads, you are modeling for your children in a little "g" god-like way, and your model is how they will see God in the future. There are serious trade-offs in your life to consider when thinking about the importance of your career compared to being present in the lives of your children.

The more we learn to be there for our kids, the more we're also showing them the heart of the Father. Our time spent on the floor playing with them, going on vacations with them, watching them from the stands—will allow the Lord to capture our hearts; consequently, we will capture the heart of our kids. I can tell you that I've been smitten.

Do You Like Me, Dad?

Do your kids think that you like them? I had the opportunity this year to sit down with about 100 young men at an event in Southern California. I asked this question: How many of you know that your dads love you? The room got quite. Most of their hands were raised. Then I asked, "How many of your dads tell you that they love you weekly?" Only a few hands went up in the room.

Then I asked, "How many of your dads are happy and like where you are in your life right now?" Only one hand went up in the room. When I pressed them further, they told me that the only time that their dads spend time with them is when he is trying to improve them.

I then asked them what they would change if they could change one thing about their dad in this area? One brave soul stood up and said, "I wish my dad would stop screaming at me and making me do what he thinks is best for me. He doesn't listen to me or care what I think." Another man said, "I just don't know if my dad likes me or if I will ever be good enough." My heart broke, and at that moment I began to recall how many of my own conversations were motivated on improving my kids and not loving them in ways that say, "I see you and believe in you."

It is far easier to stay shallow with my kids than make

myself vulnerable to them and be known. Yet there is nothing sweeter in life than knowing that you have your kids' hearts and they know you are crazy about them. What my kids want is not just my expertise or my stories—they want me and my heart. They want to know if I like them, if I am proud of them, and they pick it up through my looks, my questions and my presence.

Have you ever pulled back and distanced yourself because your kids are struggling through something? Have you ever been frustrated or hurt by someone and when you get near them, you use the silent treatment? I have. When they ask if anything is wrong, you cower and say, "I'm fine."

Have you found God that petty? I haven't. I need Him the most when I am broken. I am so grateful that He never says, "Go away, Ed. I'm too busy to listen to you." I was with a young man this week who told me that he and his dad had an argument eight years ago and have not spoken since. I looked at him and said, "Maybe it is time for the person who is the most mature to go and ask for forgiveness."

Maybe it is time for you to go and make a difference. God will back you up.

The Difference a Mom Can Make

Moms play an equally important role in this process as

well. One of the other top five questions I'm asked by people is this: How does a single mom help her kids embrace
God's unconditional love and acceptance? How does her
role differ? One of the things I see over and over again is a
mom trying to be both mother and father—and she really
can't. She feels helpless against the testosterone growth of
her son and her inability to control or lead him. Or she's just
not sure how to handle her wild daughter who shuts herself
in her room. What is a single mom to do when there's no
man around the house?

I've learned there is nothing more powerful than a
woman who has experienced the power of God's blessing
and caught the smile of the Father over her life. There is
also nothing more powerless than a woman who tries to be
the man in her kids' lives. I have sat with many tearful moms
who were frustrated and overwhelmed by trying to do the
job of two parents.

What is the answer for moms who constantly donate
their tonsils because they cannot yell loud enough? I have
found there is more power in affirmation than volume. The
answer comes in two parts. The first has to do with the way
you speak into the lives of your kids. The second has to do
with learning to trust that God is a Father to the fatherless.

If you're a single mom reading this book right now,
know that God promises to be the Father of the fatherless

(Psalm 68:5) He will become that father for your kids. You can trust that notion. I don't say that lightly. I know how deep the wound is for many moms. Though I lost my dad, my mother's prayers, her consistent manner of speaking life into me and pursuit of my Father in heaven shaped my journey. Moms can assist in this process by speaking encouraging words into the lives of their children and reminding them about God's plan and direction for their lives. It is hard to do that when you see that your kids are living from the wound of not having a dad's consistency in their lives.

I have learned a powerful thing from my mother-in-law, Nancy, who we call "Grandma Dearie." She has the practice of writing notes to all of the kids in her family and yours truly. Her notes have touched me deeply these past 25 years of marriage to her daughter. She has an uncanny ability to connect to what God has made me for and she writes it to love me. Grandma Dearie love notes have never been about her. She has never used them to vent, but they have been heartfelt glimpses of what she receives by catching God's smile for me. I feel God's pleasure for me every time she puts pen to paper.

When is the last time you wrote a note to your kids to speak life into them and to affirm them? I can hear some of you saying, "Ed, you don't understand! My son is driving me crazy! Write him a note? I'm ready to lock him up in his room." To use the words of my oldest daughter: "I feel you!" Forgiveness and a written note might be a better way. That is the way Jesus captured you.

But God demonstrates his own love for us in this: While we were still sinners, Christ died for us. (Romans 5:8, NIV)

He wrote us a love letter long before we were ready to receive Him. He spoke promises into our lives when we were at our worst. Now it's your turn. Start writing!

Build Structures to Help Dreams Come True

Ilene Bazine, the dean of the business school at Azusa Pacific University, shared with me her school's unique program that helps incoming students customize the course of their studies. While reflecting upon this unique academic plan, I thought, *Why don't we do that for our kids? Why don't we find the right fit for our kids based on how uniquely wired they are by God?*

How many of you are in jobs where you're doing something you're not made to do? You're in a sales job and you hate sales. I've met people who have spent their life doing what they're not made to do. In helping our kids experience God's love and acceptance, we must build things around them that highlight who God has called them to be on earth.

With my kids I have filled different roles in their lives to help them discover what God has called them to do, and to help them grow into it. For my oldest son, Edward, it wasn't as hard because he knew from a young age that he wanted to play professional golf. It simply required my time to be a caddy, a coach, a friend, a cheerleader, and an avid fan. I had a front row seat to watch him fulfill this first season as a pro golfer. It required getting up early to take him to the golf course, walking him through the different courses and helping him at the level that he wanted from me.

That has been some of the sweetest relationship that I could have with my son. He considers me his friend as well as his dad. I think I have learned more from him than I have taught him. Much of what I have learned about being a good dad has come from struggles Edward and I have worked through and overcome. When I started this journey on being a father, I thought I had to have all the answers. I wanted a paint-by-numbers approach. It is not that way. It is more like Van Gogh where you get paint everywhere. It can be messy sometimes, but if you stay close to your kids' hearts, the Father in Heaven puts the finishing touches on the painting we started and creates a masterpiece. If you've got paint all over you, you're in the game.

What My Girls Wanted

My oldest daughter Jessica is incredibly creative and beautiful. She's a jazz singer at heart with a passion for the broken and underprivileged—and her needs were entirely different. Her nickname was "Jukebox" when she was a little girl. She would dress up and stand out in the atrium on a rock and start performing for my attention. As soon as I paid attention and became a fan, she would run in and change her outfit and come out with a different song. I loved those days, though it was hard to get anything done while being a "Jukebox" groupie.

It took me longer to connect with Jessica. I put so much time in Edward's golf career that there was a season where she felt wounded because I was gone so much. I have learned that girls require a different level of sensitivity than boys. Jessica learned how to be more independent because I was so busy during that season. Being there for my girls required so much more of my attention.

Jessica is in college at UCLA fulfilling her dreams, and we have spent more time connecting recently. I see so much of myself in her. I am proud of the woman she has become. She is tender, loving and fights for those who feel invisible. She has taught me to see the treasure in people who are broken.

The structure for my girls started the same. They

needed regular daddy times and dates. And they needed a consistent listening ear, where I stay committed to not trying to fix them. Over the years I've learned listening and understanding keeps a woman's heart open. I wish I could say that I have perfected that skill. Wrong! All three of the women in my house are very skilled in correcting my feeble attempts at improving them. If you have your girls' hearts, you can lead them. But if you don't get their hearts and still try to lead them, you are headed for disaster.

I have known many dads who missed that opportunity because they did not know their daughters wanted them in their lives that way. Recently, a father came up to me and said, "I have been married two times and had numerous girlfriends and never knew that women and my daughters wanted a relationship with me." Guess what? Even if you have missed the first part of their dreams, it is never too late.

What Mary Wants

My daughter Mary Lee is the third woman in my house who brings the stage into every moment of life. Her heart is for song and drama, for true love and beauty. She's both beautiful and brilliant at the same time. When Mary walks in the room, it changes. She is the funniest person to work with; I feel like I am with Julie Andrews and we are living in Austria and singing *The Sound of Music* when we work together. As a matter of fact, that is our favorite album, and we play it in the office all the time.

She loves to sit and talk and ask questions. And it could come at midnight or early in the morning. She is wired so passionately that she needs me to be available to talk and help her think through her choices. I read a great article about our different learning styles, which said some learn by talking through what they think. It would irritate me that girls were so confusing! I could hear myself saying with Professor Higgins, "Why can't women be more like men?"

Mary has taught me to listen and wait for the last line of the song. Learning the art of asking the right questions helps her communicate the passion in her heart. Sometimes girls just need a shoulder to lean on because they don't know how to verbalize their feelings. Mary has shown me how powerful it is to stay present with my affirmation and smile.

Joshua, my youngest son, lives life to the fullest. He still believes everything is possible, and he's so fun to be with. He is not afraid of anything. He was pitching recently in a little league game and the league home run leader came to the plate. I was standing behind home plate, and Joshua's look changed from a smile. He became intense as he aimed the next two pitches at the batter's head. The batter had to hit the dirt twice to miss being hit by the ball. After the game, I asked him what happened. He said, "Dad, that guy laughed at me and started yelling at me, so I taught him a lesson before I struck him out. "

He made me laugh. At 10 years old his warrior heart caused him to stand. The Smile of the Father also helps us stand when we are taunted and attacked.

Each one of my kids is unique in who God has created them to be. When your heart is captured by God the Father, you'll catch His heart for your kids. It won't be about trying to get them to do your dreams—their journey with you will be sweet because you'll have their heart. Remember parents, you can't lead your kids if you don't have their hearts. You can have the best principles in life; you can have the best programs and send them to the best schools; but if you lose your kids' hearts in the journey, it will be the most painful memory you take away from being a parent. Many parents I meet feel like they blew it. But it's never too late to go back and capture your child's heart once again.

Helping Friends Embrace God's Blessing

Whether or not you're a parent, you also have the opportunity to help your friends embrace the power of God's blessing. Ask yourself this question: Who are the people you love being around the most? Usually, it's those people who aren't trying to change you, but they "feel you." They're connected with your struggles; they know who you are, and they're willing to be back-to-back with you, supporting you.

Serving as a singles pastor for a number of years gave me some unique insights about friendships. I found that those who felt stuck and alone came to be that way not because they didn't want friends, but because they were constantly looking for someone to be a friend to them first.

The way to give away the smile of the Father is to really catch the heart of the Father for those around you who you can love and serve and give yourself to. You should try to be the kind of person you would want to spend time with. Wouldn't it be great to be around people who aren't constantly manipulating you and wanting your time, people who simply want to be a part of your life?

The youth pastor in our church has given himself to spending time with a single mom's son who has no man in his life. And that boy has turned his life around, moving from a place of incredible insecurity to waiting for Jake to arrive. Jake has modeled the smile of the Father for that young boy—and he will never be the same. To have a great friend, you have to give your life away and be a great friend.

Helping Strangers Embrace God's Love

One of the most challenging and exciting parts of living in a place where you are experiencing the power of God's blessing is when you meet new people. It's exciting to demonstrate the reality of God's gifts that are inside of you to someone who has so little hope. I love those moments when you're able to represent the God of Heaven in a way that makes others understand and realize that Jesus Christ is the Son of God. It's simply priceless.

I love doing this so much that Edward recently asked me, "Dad, do you ever just go out just to play golf? Do you always have to share Christ with someone? A caddy? A teammate?" To which I answered, "Sure, if there's no one who needs to be touched or loved." He's now come to accept that in me because he understands my heart. When you know your Father in Heaven is smiling over your life, you get to see people the way God does and a stranger is not someone to be afraid of anymore. You find yourself bolder and more compassionate because God's compassion and gaze lead you to people who are hurting and broken.

I find it far more effective in sharing my faith to remember one thing that Jesus modeled throughout his ministry, and that was this: He was willing to be or do anything that needed to be done so that the other person could come to know the love God the Father had bestowed upon Him. It's why Jesus said, "I didn't come to condemn the world." He actually came to take our place and become the Savior to the world.

Give It All Away

"Freely you received, freely give," Jesus told His disciples. That's the heart of God when it comes to walking in His Kingdom. That's what it looks like to be in step with Jesus—we're simply giving away whatever God puts in our hands. When we begin to catch God's smile over our lives and experience the power of His blessing, we can't help but give it away. We want the world to know how God's love freed our soul—and how it can free theirs, too!

I pray that the message of this book has deeply impacted you. I hope your view of God has changed—and that you see Him as a loving Father, anxious for you to know Him simply because He's in love with you. Living a life that's connected to God is not about working hard to make Him proud as much as it is about opening up your soul and allowing Him to love you—and you loving Him in return. Once you catch God's Smile over your life, you can't help but reflect it.

From the Author

Once you've experienced the Power of the Blessing, it's only natural to want to pass it on.

Were you blessed by this book?
Like to help spread the word?
Want to join the team?

To become a cheerleader, visit us at
www.PowerOfTheBlessing.com
where you can:
• Sign up for our monthly newsletter
• Send a blessing to those you love
• Find Ed Tandy McGlasson's latest books
• Send books to your pastor and friends
• Acquire books in quantity for distribution
• Support our ministry by becoming a financial partner
• Bring a conference to your city
• Find resources for producing your own conference

Or drop us a note at:
fathers@mac.com